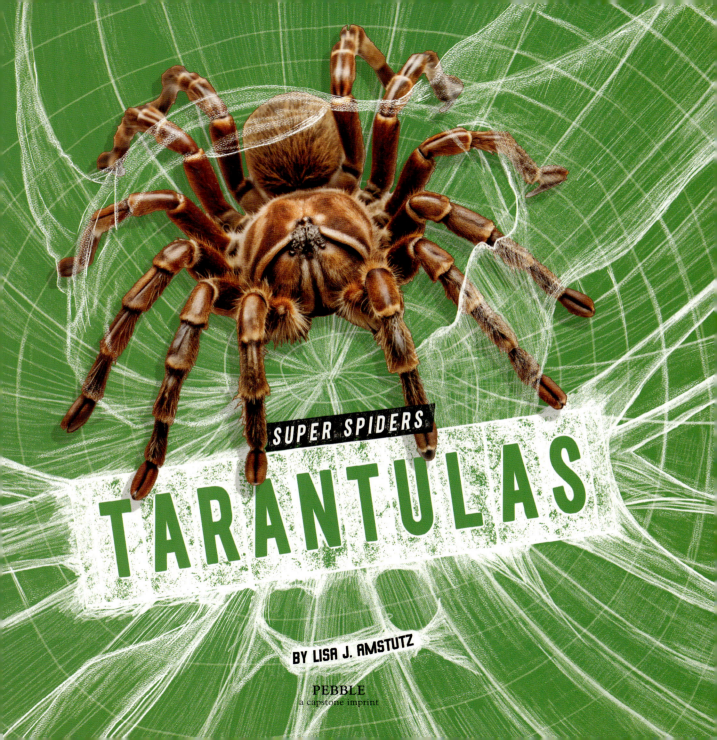

SUPER SPIDERS

TARANTULAS

BY LISA J. AMSTUTZ

PEBBLE
a capstone imprint

Published by Pebble, an imprint of Capstone
1710 Roe Crest Drive, North Mankato, Minnesota 56003
www.capstonepub.com

Copyright © 2026 by Capstone. All rights reserved. No part of this publication may be reproduced in whole or in part, or stored in a retrieval system, or transmitted in any form or by any means, electronic, mechanical, photocopying, recording, or otherwise, without written permission of the publisher.

Library of Congress Cataloging-in-Publication Data is available on the Library of Congress website.
ISBN: 9798875224836 (hardcover)
ISBN: 9798875224522 (paperback)
ISBN: 9798875224799 (ebook PDF)

Summary: An introduction to tarantulas, including where they live, what their bodies look like, how they hunt their prey, and more.

Editorial Credits
Editor: Ashley Kuehl; Designer: Bobbie Nuytten; Media Researcher: Svetlana Zhurkin; Production Specialist: Whitney Schaefer

Image Credits
Capstone: Kay Fraser (spiderweb), cover and throughout; Getty Images: Mitch Diamond, 19, Oxford Scientific, 16, Vaara, 7; Shutterstock: All Write studio (spiderweb), 4, 10, 14, Andrea Mangoni, 13, Cornel Constantin, 17, KritsadaPetchuay, 15, Maryna Lipatova, 18, PetlinDmitry, 4, reptiles4all, 6, Ryan M. Bolton, 12, Tanveer Anjum Towsif (spider), cover, back cover, 1, xtotha, 9, SuperStock: Frank Lane Picture Agency, 11, Minden Pictures, 8, 14; Svetlana Zhurkin: 20; USFWS: Gary Peeples, 5

Any additional websites and resources referenced in this book are not maintained, authorized, or sponsored by Capstone. All product and company names are trademarks™ or registered® trademarks of their respective holders.

Printed and bound in China. 6274

TABLE OF CONTENTS

Meet the Tarantula 4

Hairy Hunters 10

Furry Families 14

    Make a Spider Ring 20

    Spider Jokes 21

    Glossary 22

    Read More 23

    Internet Sites 23

    Index 24

    About the Author 24

Words in **bold** are in the glossary.

MEET THE TARANTULA

Can you imagine a spider as big as a dinner plate? Meet the Goliath birdeater! It is a type of tarantula. Others in this family are as small as your fingernail. They live in warm places around the world. Many live in South America.

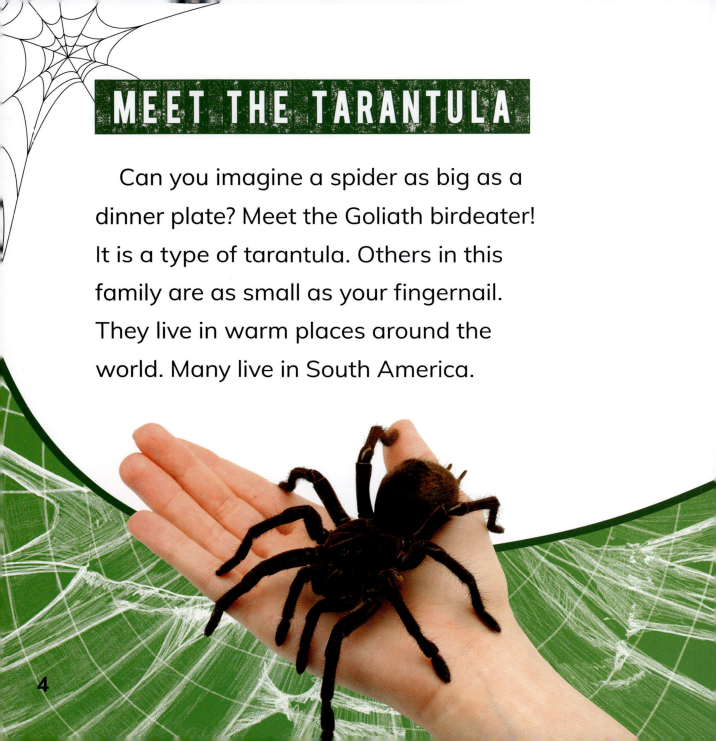

Tarantulas are very hairy. They have two body parts and eight legs. Most have eight eyes. **Organs** on their back end make **silk**.

Tarantulas live alone. They make homes in holes, under rocks, or in tree bark. Silk webs line their **burrows**.

Look out! Here comes a **predator**. Lizards, snakes, and birds eat tarantulas. One predator is a large wasp. It is called a tarantula hawk.

The spiders fight back by biting. Some can flick hairs at predators. These hairs have stinging **barbs**. They land in an animal's eyes and nose. They itch and burn.

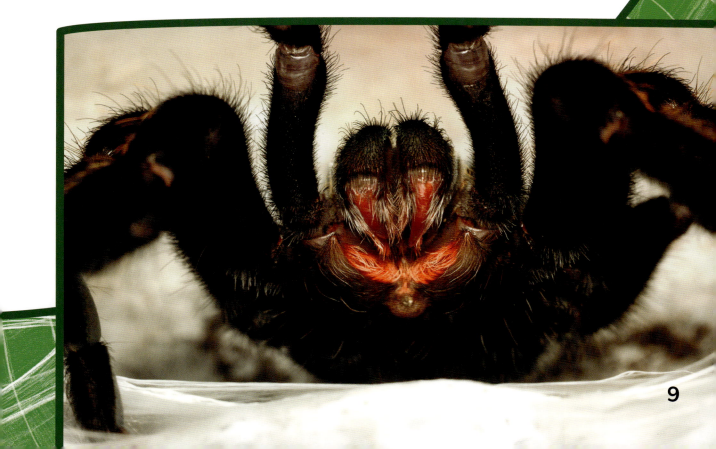

HAIRY HUNTERS

As night falls, tarantulas wake. They sit and wait for **prey** to wander by. A mouse runs past. Pounce! The spider leaps. Its strong legs grab the mouse. *Zing!* It sinks in its **fangs**.

Venom kills the mouse. Its body starts to break down. The spider can slurp out the insides. It drags its prey into its burrow to eat.

Tarantulas eat bugs and other spiders. They eat lizards, frogs, and mice too. Some even eat birds or bird eggs. A big meal can last a long time. The spider may not need to eat for a month!

FURRY FAMILIES

It is time to have babies! A male looks for a female. He follows her smell. The pair does a dance. If she likes him, they will mate.

The female makes a silk cocoon. She fills it with up to 1,000 eggs! She keeps them safe for six to nine weeks. At last, young spiders hatch. They stay nearby for two to three weeks. Then they leave home.

As the young spider grows, it **molts**. It makes a silk mat. Then it flips on its back. Its skin splits down its back. The spider stretches. The skin comes off.

The spider has brand-new skin. It waits for the new skin to harden. Then it flips over again. The spider may even regrow lost legs!

Tarantulas are fun to watch. Some people keep these spiders as pets. They feed them bugs or mice. But be careful. A tarantula bite hurts! It feels like a bee sting. But it will not kill you.

MAKE A SPIDER RING

What You Need:
- 4 pipe cleaners
- 2 pom-poms
- glue
- 2 googly eyes

What You Do:

1. Hold all 4 pipe cleaners together. Then fold them in half.

2. Twist the folded end into a loop. You will have a loop with 8 pieces sticking out.

2. Bend the pipe cleaners down to form legs.

3. Glue pom-poms on top.

4. Add googly eyes.

20

SPIDER JOKES

How tall are spiders?

Eight feet!

What did the spider say to the fly?

Buzz off!

Why did the spider put one leg out of bed?

She wanted to start the day on the right foot!

What do you call a sneaky tarantula?

a spy-der

GLOSSARY

barb (BAHRB)—a tiny, pointy hook

burrow (BUR-oh)—a hole in the ground made or used by an animal

fang (FANG)—the biting part of a spider's mouth

molt (MOHLT)—to shed an outer layer of skin

organ (OR-guhn)—a part of the body that has a special job

predator (PRED-uh-tur)—an animal that hunts other animals for food

prey (PRAY)—an animal hunted by another animal for food

silk (SILK)—long, thin threads made by a spider

venom (VEN-uhm)—a poisonous liquid produced by some animals

READ MORE

Becker, Trudy. *Tarantulas*. Lake Elmo, MN: Focus Readers, 2023.

Bow, James. *Tarantulas*. Mendota Heights, MN: Apex Editions, 2024.

Humphrey, Natalie. *Goliath Bird-Eating Spiders*. Buffalo, NY: Gareth Stevens Publishing, 2025.

INTERNET SITES

Britannica Kids: Tarantula
kids.britannica.com/kids/article/tarantula/353837

National Geographic Kids: Tarantula
kids.nationalgeographic.com/animals/invertebrates/facts/tarantula

National Wildlife Federation: Tarantulas
nwf.org/Educational-Resources/Wildlife-Guide/Invertebrates/Tarantulas

INDEX

barbs, 9
biting, 9, 18
burrows, 7, 10

fangs, 10

legs, 6, 10, 17

mating, 14
molting, 16

pets, 18
predators, 8, 9

silk, 6, 7, 15, 16

size, 4

venom, 10

webs, 7

ABOUT THE AUTHOR

Lisa Amstutz is the author of more than 150 children's books on topics ranging from applesauce to zebra mussels. An ecologist by training, she enjoys sharing her love of nature with kids. Lisa lives on a small farm with her family.